TRANS FORMERS
THE ULTIMATE GUIDE

Licensed By:

TRANSFORMERS © 2011 Hasbro. All Rights Reserved.

© 2011 Paramount Pictures Corporation. All Rights Reserved.

978-0-00-742868-7

1 3 5 7 9 10 8 6 4 2

First published in the UK by HarperCollins Children's Books in 2011

A CIP catalogue record for this title is available from the British Library.

HOOVER DAM ROBOT ATTACKS

A giant robot rampaged through Mission City today, destroying cars, buildings and causing $5 million of damage to a skyscraper. The giant monster is believed to have escaped from a military compound in the Hoover Dam, and was only defeated with the help of several other giant robot warriors. Military sources are keeping quiet but the monster's

The Hoover Dam beast pictured yesterday

VICTORIAN TIMES · 4th March 1897

ICE MONSTER REVEALED

Arctic explorer Captain Archibald Witwicky claims to have made an important discovery this week during his exploration of the Arctic Circle. His team uncovered what they claim is a giant, possibly extra-terrestrial ro-bot frozen in the ice. They told reporters that the robot has been there for hundreds, if not thousands, of years. It seems Captain Witwicky's imagination has finally got

FALLEN TO 'RISE AGAIN'

Military sources from NEST have played down reports in the media that a new, sinister threat to Earth is about to appear. During a routine mission in Shanghai, NEST Autobot leader Optimus Prime destroyed two Decepticon enemies in battle. Witnesses report that one of the Decepticons, known as Demolishor, cried, 'The Fallen will rise again!' as he was defeated. Who or what 'The Fallen' is remains to be seen.

DECEPTICONS HOLD WORLD TO RANSOM

Armies all over the world were on red alert yesterday as the Decepticons issued their clearest threat yet to the human race. They are demanding that a certain American called Sam Witwicky be handed over to them, or they will unleash more of the terrible violence that has been seen over the past week. Sources in the US army say that they have no idea where Witwicky is, but that he is in grave danger and should contact them immediately.

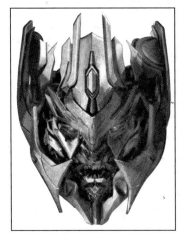

Decepticon leader Megatron on TV yesterday

'FALLEN' FALLS AS AUTOBOTS SAVE DAY

The Decepticon threat to Earth was removed for good yesterday as the Autobot forces, alongside NEST, successfully prevented Decepticon leader The Fallen from activating his Star Harvester and destroying our solar system. Autobot leader Optimus Prime is believed to have made the final attack, and while witnesses report that The Fallen was killed, the whereabouts of Megatron is unknown.

The Fallen pictured at the pyramids in Egypt just before the battle started

ROGUE DECEPTICON
SAVES DAY

An old Decepticon called Jetfire is believed to have played a key role in defeating The Fallen last week, according to new witnesses who saw the epic battle in Egypt. Jetfire is believed to have switched sides and joined the Autobots, and in a final sacrifice allowed Optimus Prime to use his parts, giving him the strength to kill The Fallen. Sources said "Jetfire's sacrifice will be remembered

Optimus Prime

ROBOTS IN EXILE

The Autobots fled their home planet of Cybertron after it was ravaged by civil war. They arrived on Earth seeking the AllSpark, an object which could rebuild their planet, allowing them to live in peace again.

AUTOBOTS VS. DECEPTICONS

The Autobots should not be confused with their Decepticon enemies. While both factions were at war on Cybertron, the Autobots seek a peaceful end to the war and want to use the AllSpark to revive their planet. The Decepticons, however, see it as the first step to ruling the universe.

HUMAN PROTECTORS

Despite their fearsome appearance, the Autobots have always shown themselves to be very protective of humans. Their continued presence here is due to their desire to protect the human race from the Decepticons. As the Star Harvester incident proves, we are very reliant on this protection.

NEST

The Autobots, under leader Optimus Prime, have been working with the military at NEST to monitor the Decepticon threat and to extinguish it where possible. Their role is crucial as human weaponry is no match for the Decepticons.

4

CIVIL WAR

Megatron and the Decepticons began the civil war that destroyed Cybertron, when they grouped together to steal the AllSpark. Megatron saw it as his route to complete power: only Optimus Prime and the Autobots have stopped him reaching his goal so far.

THE FIGHT CONTINUES

Despite Cybertron's fate, the war has continued, as the Decepticons see Earth as crucial to restoring their planet and power. They have sought the AllSpark here; they have tried to destroy our sun to harvest its energy; and they have tried to enslave the human race and use Earth as a resource to rebuild their planet. They have no regard at all for human life.

COMMAND STRUCTURE

The Decepticons answer to their leader Megatron, who first sought absolute power on Cybertron. He has a strong dislike of humans, since they imprisoned him at Hoover Dam. He ultimately answered to The Fallen, a very ancient member of the Primes, but since The Fallen's death, Megatron is the true Decepticon leader.

CONTINUED THREAT

It is very unlikely that the Decepticons will give up their quest for power and I recommend a permanent Autobot presence on Earth, to protect against possible further attacks.

OPTIMUS PRIME

KEY FACTS

LEADER OF THE AUTOBOTS

LAST OF THE PRIMES

UNSTOPPABLE STRENGTH

INSPIRATIONAL CHIEF

Optimus Prime is the last of the Primes – or so he thought, until he encountered The Fallen and Sentinel Prime, both also members of this ancient Transformer family.

As leader of the Autobots, Optimus led them to Earth in the first place, to protect the planet from the Decepticons – and to find the AllSpark to help rebuild Cybertron.

Optimus is the only Transformer big and strong enough to take on Megatron – and the two robots have had several epic battles.

Optimus was actually killed by Megatron once – only to be revived by Sam using the Matrix of Leadership.

Optimus leads by example. He is always first into battle and his bravery is an inspiration to the other Autobots.

Optimus holds the Matrix of Leadership in his chest. This means he can bring other Transformers back to life. The Matrix can only be held by a Prime.

Optimus is determined to save Earth from the Decepticons, and will fight to the death to keep the human race free.

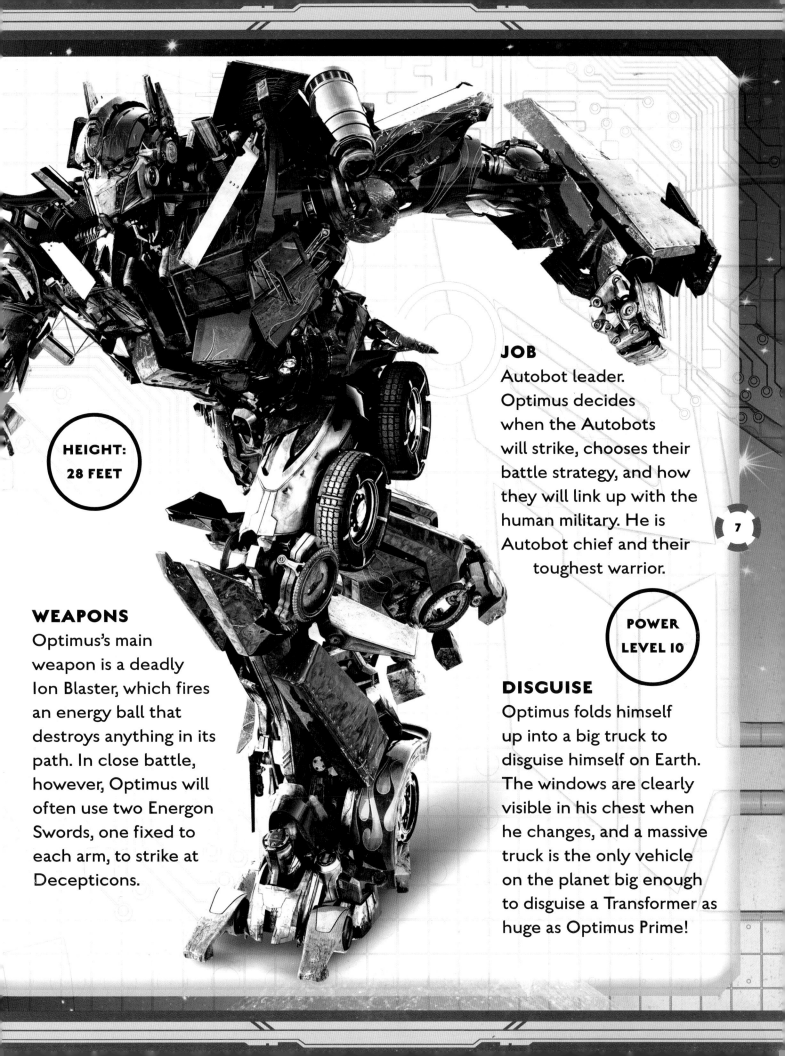

HEIGHT: 28 FEET

JOB
Autobot leader. Optimus decides when the Autobots will strike, chooses their battle strategy, and how they will link up with the human military. He is Autobot chief and their toughest warrior.

WEAPONS
Optimus's main weapon is a deadly Ion Blaster, which fires an energy ball that destroys anything in its path. In close battle, however, Optimus will often use two Energon Swords, one fixed to each arm, to strike at Decepticons.

POWER LEVEL 10

DISGUISE
Optimus folds himself up into a big truck to disguise himself on Earth. The windows are clearly visible in his chest when he changes, and a massive truck is the only vehicle on the planet big enough to disguise a Transformer as huge as Optimus Prime!

MEGATRON

KEY FACTS

LEADER OF THE DECEPTICONS

DEADLY WARRIOR

OPTIMUS PRIME'S MAIN RIVAL

ENEMY OF HUMAN RACE

Megatron is the most powerful and deadly Decepticon, and is a dangerous and determined leader. When he is on a mission, nothing except Optimus Prime can stop him!

Megatron and Optimus have met several times in epic hand-to-hand battles. Megatron is bigger than Optimus and has beaten him several times, but Optimus usually finishes on top.

Megatron wants the AllSpark just as much as Optimus does. But rather than using it to regenerate Cybertron for peaceful purposes, Megatron would use it to rule the universe!

Megatron's hatred of the human race stems from the thousands of years he spent frozen in ice at the North Pole, after crashing there during the last Ice Age – before being discovered by Sector 7.

Megatron hates being ruled, and turns on Sentinel Prime when he realises Sentinel intends to rule Cybertron by himself. Megatron wants to beat the Autobots his way – or not at all!

WEAPONS

Megatron has an ion-fused chain whip, which he can swing at enemies with deadly force. He also has an arm cannon, and a fearsome death-lock pincer on his arm that can slice through enemies at close range.

JOB

Leader of the Decepticons and the brains behind their attacks. He can work for greater powers, such as The Fallen or Sentinel Prime, but prefers to be his own boss and run things his way.

DISGUISE

Megatron changes into a Cybertronian winged tank, which can be used as a battle vehicle, and can also fly unaided into space – making Megatron quick into battle, and very hard to destroy. He can turn into a Cybetronian attack jet, a Cybertronian tank, and an Earth-based oil tanker truck.

HEIGHT: 35 FEET

POWER LEVEL 10

CYBERTRON AND THE CIVIL WAR

The Decepticons and the Autobots have been at war since long before they landed on Earth. It all began on their home planet, Cybertron...

A STRUGGLE FOR POWER

Once upon a time, Cybertron was ruled peacefully by the Primes, and there were no factions among the Transformers. The key to power lay in the AllSpark, which could bring life to Transformers. However, the Decepticons weren't happy to share power with the Autobots, and wanted to rule Cybertron alone.

THE RISE OF THE AUTOBOTS

Optimus Prime gathered the Autobots around him to fight the Decepticon forces, and preserve freedom on Cybertron. But both sides were strong, and the war dragged on. Eventually, the war-torn planet was all but destroyed – a desolate wasteland, ruled over by the Decepticons, with a few Autobots still fighting for freedom.

THE FIGHT LEAVES CYBERTRON

As Cybertron became increasingly ruined, the fight left the planet – and came to Earth. The chase for the AllSpark led here – and with it Decepticons who wanted to use it to gain victory, and Autobots seeking to protect freedom. Earth was initially a side-show to the war – but has ended up being the key battle ground for Transformer power.

THE REBUILDING OF CYBERTRON

Whoever wins the war will have to rebuild Cybertron, ravaged after centuries of war and destruction. The Decepticons see Earth as a disposable way to rebuild Cybertron – either by harvesting Earth's sun (as The Fallen attempted), or by using humans as slaves (as Sentinel Prime wanted to do using the Space Bridge). Only the Autobots stand up for the human race and insist that other planets should not be harmed.

THE WAR CONTINUES

As long as Megatron seeks ultimate power, Optimus and the Autobots will be there to stop him. Now that the fight has moved to Earth, the Autobots are essential to the survival of the planet.

KEY CYBERTRONIAN OBJECTS

The AllSpark – This powerful device was the key to power on Cybertron. It could bring Transformers to life, and gave its owner ultimate power on Cybertron. The chase for the AllSpark led to the huge battle in Mission City. Sam used the AllSpark to kill Megatron, destroying it in the process.

The Matrix of Leadership – Optimus Prime carries the Matrix in his chest. It can give life to Transformers, and it is only ever possessed by a Prime and the leader of the Autobots. It was a key part of the battle of the Star Harvester, as it can activate the Harvester – and it has brought Optimus, Sentinel and Sam back to life.

The Space Bridge – This vast teleportation device was designed to help the Autobots win the war or escape Cybertron, but it fell into Decepticon hands thanks to Sentinel Prime's betrayal. It was almost used to turn Earth into a slave planet – but the Autobots destroyed it at the last minute.

The Star Harvester – This tool was used in ancient times to destroy suns, creating Energon to power Cybertron. Only The Fallen was willing to destroy a sun that supported life, though – our sun – leading to a rift with the Primes, and a huge battle with the Autobots 17,000 years later.

TRANSFORMERS TIMELINE

ANCIENT HISTORY

● Cybertron at peace

● Dynasty of Primes sets out to find suns to harvest

● The Fallen tries to harvest Earth's sun: Other Primes stop him, hide Matrix of Leadership in their tomb

● Cybertron descends into war as Decepticons try to seize power

● Cybertron increasingly ravaged as civil war continues

● Optimus sends the AllSpark out into space to stop Decepticons getting it

● AllSpark lands on Earth

● Last Ice Age: Megatron crash - lands on Earth, is frozen in ice

PRESENT DAY

- Starscream and Decepticons arrive on Earth, free Megatron
- Autobots arrive to stop Decepticons getting AllSpark
- Battle at Mission City sees AllSpark destroyed
- The Fallen returns to Earth to complete harvesting of sun
- Sam discovers Matrix of Leadership hidden in Tomb of Primes
- Battle at the Pyramid sees Matrix returned to Optimus, Fallen killed
- Optimus discovers Ark and revives Sentinel Prime
- Decepticons activate Space Bridge
- Cybertron briefly appears in Earth's atmosphere
- Optimus and Megatron defeat Sentinel
- Autobots remain on Earth to protect humans

MODERN HISTORY

- Sentinel Prime escapes Cybertron with Space Bridge
- 1897: Megatron discovered by Captain Archibald Witwicky
- Megatron and AllSpark kept in Hoover Dam by Sector 7
- 1960s: Sentinel's ship, the Ark, crash-lands on moon
- 1969: Americans land on moon, discover wreck of Ark

BUMBLEBEE

KEY FACTS

AUTOBOT SCOUT

SAM'S PERSONAL BODYGUARD

INCREDIBLY LOYAL

TALKS THROUGH RADIO AS VOICE

BOX DAMAGED

Bumblebee's first job on Earth was tracking down Sam and keeping him safe. He's stuck by Sam's side ever since to protect him from the Decepticons.

Bumblebee was captured by Sector 7 when he first revealed himself. Luckily, Sam persuaded them that he was a good guy, and he was released to fight alongside the army unit.

Though having an Autobot bodyguard is useful, it can be a challenge too... when protecting Sam from tiny Decepticons in his kitchen, Bumblebee almost destroyed the entire house!

Bumblebee's voice box was damaged in battle, so he has learnt to communicate by patching together words and songs from his car radio.

Bumblebee proves his strength in battle time and again, including ripping Rampage and Ravage in half during the battle for the Star Harvester in Egypt.

JOB

Autobot scout and Sam's bodyguard. Because of the Decepticon threat to Sam, Optimus agreed that Bumblebee can stay with him to protect him, and he lives in Sam's garage.

DISGUISE

Chevrolet Camaro. Bumblebee's first disguise was an old, battered 1970s model – but he soon upgraded to a cool new Camaro model, which Sam is very pleased about!

WEAPONS

Bumblebee has twin plasma cannons for use in battle, as well as electric stingers on each arm for close combat. He is strong for his size too, ripping Ravage and Rampage in half with his bare hands.

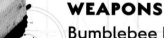

HEIGHT:
16.2 FEET

POWER
LEVEL 6

SKIDS & MUDFLAP

SKIDS

JOB
Autobot warrior. Skids provides backup alongside Mudflap when the Autobots roll into battle.

WEAPONS
Powerful right arm can smash Decepticons apart, and matches Mudflap's powerful left arm. Also has psychic link with Mudflap.

DISGUISE
Green Chevrolet Beat concept car. This small but fast car is a perfect disguise for the junior warriors.

EXTRA FACT:
Skids thinks he is more clever and more mature than his brother, but he is just as hyperactive and likely to get into trouble!

MUDFLAP

JOB
Autobot warrior and partner to Skids. The two brothers always work as a team in battle.

WEAPONS
Powerful left arm to match Skids' powerful right arm. Also has psychic link with Skids, so the pair can launch coordinated attacks without speaking to each other.

DISGUISE
Orange Chevrolet Beat concept car that matches Skids' green one, helping them blend in with normal human traffic.

HEIGHT: 11 FEET

POWER LEVEL 4

EXTRA FACT:
Skids and Mudflap are always arguing – but it is a fight between them that leads to the discovery of the Tomb of the Primes when they crash into an ancient wall in Egypt.

THREE PRIMES

The name 'Prime' indicates a special Transformer. The Primes are an ancient race of Transformer leaders, with Optimus Prime being the current chief. But two other Primes from the past came back to join the war again...

DYNASTY OF THE PRIMES

An ancient group of Primes set off from Cybertron thousands of years ago to find suns to harvest for Energon. The Fallen was one of those Primes. He went against their rules by building a Star Harvester on a planet with life; the other Primes all sacrificed themselves to save Earth, making a tomb out of their bodies to seal the Matrix of Leadership inside. Thousands of years later, The Fallen came back to find it...

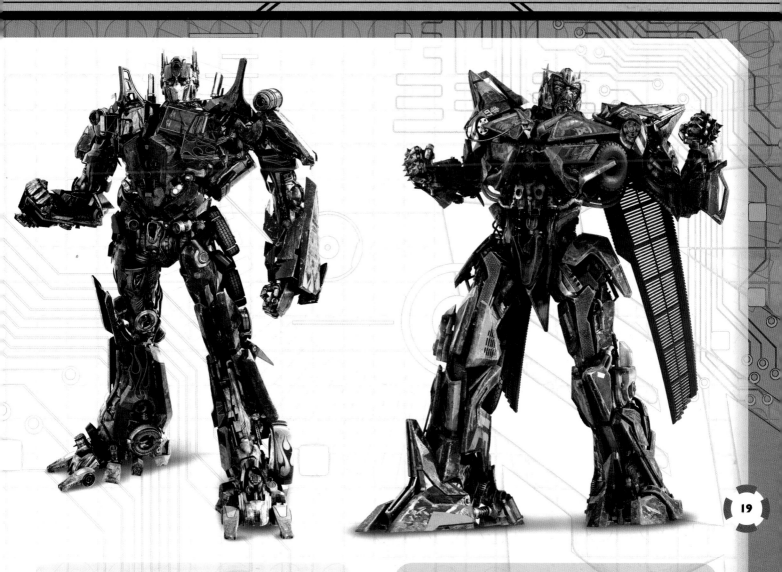

LATEST PRIME LEADER

Optimus Prime is the latest Prime to rule over the Transformers, though only the Autobots answer to him. As a Prime, Optimus has wisdom, strength, and also a special role to play in the war with the Decepticons: for example, only a Prime can kill The Fallen, so Optimus has to take on the job. Unlike The Fallen and Sentinel Prime, Optimus remains loyal to his ancestors and their vision of a peaceful, restored Cybertron.

PRIME TRAITOR

In a flashback to the Cybertron wars, Optimus sees Sentinel Prime fleeing Cybertron. He was carrying pillars for a Space Bridge away from the planet. Optimus assumes that this was to help the Autobots escape – but when Sentinel Prime arrives back on Earth, it soon becomes clear that he is a traitor. He was trying to trap the Autobots on Cybertron. It takes an unlikely partnership between Megatron and Optimus to defeat the powerful Sentinel in a final, devastating battle.

THE FALLEN

KEY FACTS

FOUNDER OF THE DECEPTICONS
ORIGINAL MEMBER OF THE PRIMES

TURNED EVIL AND BANISHED
THOUSANDS OF YEARS AGO
WANTS TO DESTROY EARTH

The Fallen was one of the original Primes, sent out from Cybertron to find suns to harvest for Energon, to keep Cybertron alive.

The Primes agreed not to harvest suns in solar systems where there was life. But The Fallen didn't care – and decided to harvest Earth's sun. He enlisted the evil Transformers to help him.

The other Primes thwarted him by sealing the Matrix of Leadership – which activates the Star Harvester – inside a tomb made of their own bodies.

17,000 years later, The Fallen wanted to come back and finish the job.

Luckily, the Autobots were protecting Earth – with Optimus, a descendent of the Primes, leading them.

As the founder of the Decepticons, The Fallen was their ultimate leader – even Megatron took orders from him.

JOB

True leader of the Decepticons. Wanted to harvest Earth's sun, using the energy to rebuild Cybertron but killing all humans in the process.

DISGUISE

The Fallen has no alternate form. He has no need to hide due to his power and the protection of the Decepticons.

WEAPONS

Huge spear. Can also unleash a devastating shockwave that kills anything in its path. The Fallen can teleport too, appearing anywhere in the world – or out of it!

HEIGHT:
42 FEET

POWER
LEVEL 10

TRANSFORMER WEAPONS

The Transformers won't share their technology with humans, but they developed terrifying weapons during the Cybertron civil war...

ENERGY ROCKET LAUNCHER

Ironhide has a ton of weapons, but the deadliest one is this powerful rocket launcher that can destroy almost anything in its path.

PLASMA CANNON

Plasma weapons are a key part of Transformer technology. Bumblebee has a devastating plasma cannon fixed into his right arm.

SPINNING SAW

It's not all about guns on Cybertron. Ratchet has a deadly spinning saw in his left arm to attack Decepticons at close range.

ARM SWORDS

Sideswipe has close-combat weapons fixed into his arms – in the form of two solid swords covering his hands.

SUCKING JAWS

A huge beast like Devastator doesn't need guns. He sucks enemies up into his enormous mouth furnace.

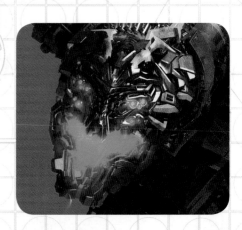

SPINNING BLADES

Blackout can use his helicopter blades as a deadly weapon when fighting at close range.

ENERGY SWORDS

This Energon sword makes Optimus incredibly fierce in close combat. He has one on each arm for extra power.

FUSION CANNON

A massive cannon sits on the end of Shockwave's arm, making him a deadly enemy. It can unleash a plasma blast powerful enough to kill an Autobot with one hit.

DISARMING TOOLS

As well as powerful guns, Jazz has a special magnet fitted to his right arm – which can disarm enemies by grabbing their guns from a distance.

RATCHET

KEY FACTS

AUTOBOT MEDICAL OFFICER

REPAIRS AUTOBOTS AFTER BATTLE

ADVISOR TO OPTIMUS

Ratchet is an essential member of the Autobot team as he is the only one who can repair damaged Autobots after battle – using special lasers.

Ratchet is essentially a peaceful Autobot, though he has to join in battles as part of the team and can be very dangerous thanks to his spinning saw arm.

He helped fuse Jetfire's parts with Optimus's body during the battle against The Fallen in Egypt, allowing Optimus to fly and finally defeat the Decepticon.

JOB

Autobot medical officer. Charged with repairing and maintaining the Autobots after battles.

WEAPONS

Spinning saw on left arm for use in close-range fighting. Also two machine guns, one in each arm, for use when further away.

DISGUISE

Ratchet changes into a large Hummer H2 search and rescue vehicle to disguise himself amongst humans.

HEIGHT: 20.1 FEET

POWER LEVEL 4

SIDESWIPE

KEY FACTS

AUTOBOT WARRIOR

ROLLS ON WHEELS FOR EXTRA SPEED

USEFUL IN HIGH-SPEED CHASES

Sideswipe's speed makes him the perfect Autobot to unleash when chasing down Decepticons. He can launch attacks while the other Autobots catch up.

Sideswipe killed Decepticon Sideways by using his huge sword arms to chop him in half, right down the middle, after a fast chase in China.

He was one of the Autobots who responded to Optimus Prime's deep-space call for more Transformers, to help him in the battle against Megatron.

Sideswipe was a key part of the huge battle for the Star Harvester in Egypt, where he took on the Decepticons with the rest of the Autobots.

JOB

Autobot warrior, who thanks to his wheeled feet is very fast and agile in chase and battle. Adds a new level to the Autobot attack team.

WEAPONS

Huge, sharp swords attached to each arm make him deadly in hand-to-hand combat with Decepticons. He is also a martial arts expert, and is at his best fighting at close range or at speed.

DISGUISE

Chevrolet Corvette. This fast, sleek car is the perfect disguise for the Autobots' speediest soldier.

HEIGHT: 20.1 FEET

POWER LEVEL 8

25

IRONHIDE

KEY FACTS

AUTOBOT WEAPONS EXPERT

EXPERIENCED WARRIOR

VERY STRONG

HEAVILY ARMED

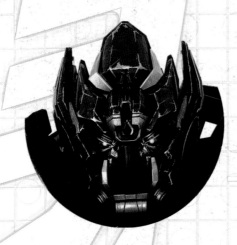

Ironhide is an ancient Autobot who has fought alongside Optimus Prime for centuries. The two trust each other completely.

While Optimus will often consider a peaceful approach, Ironhide is normally in favour of unleashing his cannons on any enemies, misbehaving pets or even annoying humans!

Ironhide's massive bulk doesn't stop him performing agile battle moves, such as twisting through the air while firing both guns.

Many Decepticons, including Brawl, Starscream and Demolishor have felt the pain of Ironhide's attack. He has battled several Decepticons at once while covering the injured Bumblebee's back.

Scars around Ironhide's eye show that the fighting on Earth is just the latest in an age-old war with the Decepticons.

JOB

Autobot weapons expert. Ironhide is very heavily armed, and a veteran warrior who can co-ordinate the rest of the Autobot team in attack when necessary.

WEAPONS

Ironhide has enormous energy rocket launchers on each arm, which can destroy a lesser robot at range. His fearsome strength makes him deadly close-up, too.

DISGUISE

GMC Topkick pick-up truck. This big, tough vehicle is large enough to disguise Ironhide and tough enough to drive him into battle!

HEIGHT:
22 FEET

POWER
LEVEL 8

THE SPACE BRIDGE

What is this mysterious Cybertronian invention – and why could it mean the end of the human race if Sentinel Prime gets his way?

WHAT DOES IT DO?

The Space Bridge teleports things through space and time, instantly. It can transport Transformers, supplies, and even a whole planet if there are enough pillars in action.

SENTINEL'S INVENTION

Sentinel Prime, while leader of the Autobots, invented the Space Bridge – and only he can activate it. He developed it to help the Autobots win the war on Cybertron, by teleporting supplies to their army, or helping Autobots to escape. But he defected to Megatron, and now plans to use the Space Bridge to win the war for the Decepticons...

ESCAPE FROM CYBERTRON

When Sentinel Prime fled Cybertron in the Ark with the Space Bridge, Optimus assumed it was to help the Autobots escape. In fact, it was to keep them trapped on Cybertron.

CRASH LANDING

Sentinel Prime and Megatron's plan failed, however, when Sentinel crash-landed on the moon. They were due to meet on Earth, but Sentinel never arrived. The Decepticons found the pillars on the moon – but they couldn't activate the Bridge without Sentinel. And he was dead!

THE REVIVAL

Without realising it, Optimus plays into Megatron's hands by reviving Sentinel Prime. Now the Decepticons can activate the Space Bridge at last! Of course, Optimus didn't know his old master was a traitor when he brought him back to life...

HOW DOES IT WORK?

Four pillars are set up in a large square. Sentinel then activates the Anchor Pillar, and the Bridge opens. The more pillars that are set up around the world, the stronger the Bridge. But the Anchor Pillar is still the key.

WHY IS EARTH IN DANGER?

The Decepticons have a daring plan for the Bridge. They want to use it to bring Cybertron to Earth! Once the planets are next to each other, they will enslave the human race, and make them rebuild Cybertron.

THE ONE WEAKNESS

The war looks lost when Sentinel activates the Space Bridge, linking thousands of pillars all over the world. But the key to the Bridge lies in one Anchor Pillar. Optimus knows this – and with a little help from Major Lennox and Epps in Chicago, the Anchor Pillar is destroyed – and Cybertron disappears from the sky.

BLACKOUT

KEY FACTS

DECEPTICON WARRIOR

CHANGES INTO HELICOPTER

DEADLY AT CLOSE RANGE

Blackout launched a single-handed attack against a military base in Qatar, and almost razed it to the ground searching for information on the AllSpark.

Blackout fought alongside Megatron in Mission City, but his attack on Sam backfires when the army get involved and bring him down with missile strikes.

His helicopter blades make a fearsome back-up weapon when he is attacking humans and Autobots.

JOB
Decepticon warrior, charged with locating and retrieving the AllSpark on Earth and helping Megatron rise to power.

DISGUISE
MH-53 Pave Low military helicopter, making Blackout airborne along with several other Decepticons.

WEAPONS
Large guns on each arm; two energy cannons for long-range destruction; spinning helicopter blades on left arm.

30

POWER
LEVEL 8

HEIGHT:
33 FEET

RAVAGE

KEY FACTS

DECEPTICON SPY & WARRIOR   BEAST-LIKE KILLER

Ravage is an animal-like Decepticon who runs like a big cat, but is ten times as deadly.

Ravage was sent to Earth to find the lost AllSpark shard. He unleashed a team of microcons to find it, by firing them out of his mouth.

Ravage was unleashed on Bumblebee in the battle for the Star Harvester, but Bumblebee used his superior strength to kill the Decepticon.

JOB

Decepticon spy, sent to find the AllSpark shard. Also joins other Decepticons in battle.

WEAPONS

Twin machine guns on back. Also sharp tail club which can whip round, and metal claws on all feet.

DISGUISE

Ravage can fold up into a smooth entry pod, to be fired onto enemy planets like Earth.

POWER LEVEL 6

31

HEIGHT:
5 FEET FROM PAW TO HEAD,
10 FEET FROM NOSE TO TAIL

SENTINEL PRIME

KEY FACTS

OLD LEADER OF THE AUTOBOTS

TRAITOR TO AUTOBOT CAUSE

MADE SECRET PACT WITH MEGATRON

CREATOR OF THE SPACE BRIDGE

Sentinel Prime was once leader of the Autobots, leading the fight against the Decepticons on Cybertron.

He invented the Space Bridge, a device that can teleport objects and people across space. It was designed to help the Autobots beat the Decepticons and rebuild Cybertron.

Sentinel gave up hope of beating the Decepticons, however, and made a secret deal with Megatron.

He would escape with the Space Bridge, meet Megatron on Earth, and the two would rebuild and rule Cybertron together.

After crash-landing on the moon, Sentinel's plans never came about – until Optimus found and revived him. Now Megatron and the Decepticons realise they could complete their scheme after all...

Sentinel was Optimus's leader and master – he taught Optimus all he knows, from battle techniques to the importance of life and freedom. Which is why Optimus is so shocked to discover that he is a traitor...

JOB

Old leader of the Autobots, now rival leader of the Decepticons with Megatron. Creator and master of the Space Bridge, and the only Transformer in the universe who can activate it.

WEAPONS

Rust Cannon, which, when blasted at a Transformer, quickly engulfs their metal parts in rust, freezing and killing them within seconds.

DISGUISE

Sentinel Prime changes into a fire truck, which is big enough to hide his great bulk, and tough enough to ride into battle. He still looks like an Autobot, even though he has deserted to join the Decepticons.

HEIGHT:
37 FEET

33

POWER
LEVEL 10

MEGA BATTLES

The fight for Earth has led to some amazing one-on-one Transformer battles. Here are some of the best and fiercest Transformer fights...

OPTIMUS PRIME VS. MEGATRON

The leaders of the warring factions have met many times in battle, but are so evenly matched that there is rarely a final victor. In Mission City, they tore at each other amongst the skyscrapers – but it took Sam's intervention to finally defeat the powerful Megatron. Optimus has lost fights too, with Megatron killing him when working for The Fallen – before Sam revived Optimus with the Matrix.

SIDESWIPE VS. SIDEWAYS

Sideswipe is chasing down Decepticons in China when he catches up with Sideways. In the fight that follows, he leaps over Sideways, and uses his arm sword to chop the Decepticon clean in half, in a battle-ending move that can't be beaten!

OPTIMUS PRIME VS. THE FALLEN

Optimus had only seconds left to destroy The Fallen before he activated the Star Harvester. As he saw his enemy scaling the Great Pyramid, the dying Jetfire made the ultimate sacrifice. He gave Optimus his jets and guns. Once Optimus was airborne, The Fallen didn't stand a chance...

MEGATRON AND OPTIMUS VS. SENTINEL PRIME

In an unlikely partnership, an enraged Megatron joins Optimus in fighting Sentinel Prime in Chicago. Optimus wants to kill Sentinel to stop him using humans as slaves to rebuild Cybertron. Megatron is furious that Sentinel is grabbing all the power for himself, when Megatron wants to rule Cybertron himself. For a moment, Megatron and Optimus want the same thing – to defeat Sentinel. And together, they do!

BUMBLEBEE VS. CROWBAR

When a trio of Decepticon Dreads attack Bumblebee, Mirage and Sideswipe, Bumblebee takes control and a high-speed battle follows. Bumblebee dispatches Crowbar with a 150mph head-on blast, before throwing Sam into the air, changing into a robot, dodging two missiles and catching Sam again as he switches back into car form!

SHOCKWAVE

KEY FACTS

LOYAL SOLDIER TO MEGATRON

RUTHLESS TO HUMANS

LOGICAL, SCIENTIFIC MIND

USES DRILLER AS A KILLER PET

Shockwave is an old and loyal servant to Megatron, fighting by his side in the Cybertronian wars. He came to Earth to join the fight against the Autobots at Megatron's command.

A clever Decepticon, Shockwave has a cold, calculating mind that shows no emotion towards either his friends or his enemies. He is focused on winning whatever the cost.

A fierce battle in Chicago sees Shockwave and Optimus go head to head. Shockwave brings Optimus down by cutting off his jet pack – but Optimus's strength sees him win the fight in the end.

SHOCKWAVE'S DRILLER

The Cybertronian Driller was traditionally used for mining back on Cybertron. Shockwave's pet, however, is five times bigger than a usual driller!

At over 100 feet long, this Driller has been modified for battle. It is equipped with guns, and its long tentacles are strong enough to kill almost anything in its path!

JOB

Decepticon warrior and commander. His keen intelligence makes Shockwave a reliable deputy for Megatron and he is entrusted with important missions.

WEAPONS

A huge fusion cannon sits at the end of Shockwave's arm, unleashing a deadly plasma blast on his enemies in battle.

DISGUISE

Shockwave has no alternate form, as he rides around on the back of his Driller.

HEIGHT: 32 FEET

POWER LEVEL 8

FRENZY

KEY FACTS

DECEPTICON SPY AND COMPUTER HACKER

SMALL AND AGILE

TECHNOLOGY WHIZZ

Frenzy is only four feet tall, but he can cause a lot of damage. His special skill is hacking into computer systems to bring down army bases.

It was Frenzy who freed Megatron when he was frozen in the Hoover Dam. He hacked into the military system and switched off the coolers keeping Megatron on ice.

Frenzy is very adaptable and can even function with his head chopped off. His head disguises itself as Mikaela's mobile phone to follow her and Sam.

JOB

Decepticon computer hacker and surveillance spy. Sent forward to find Sam, and also in charge of bringing down military base computers.

WEAPONS

Small guns on each arm, and spinning disc launcher in chest mean he can defend himself if attacked. But he is not a warrior.

DISGUISE

Boombox music player initially. But when his head is chopped off he adopts a new disguise, as Mikaela's mobile phone.

HEIGHT: 4 FEET

POWER LEVEL 2

38

JAZZ

KEY FACTS

AUTOBOT LIEUTENANT

SMALL, NIMBLE WARRIOR

FAST HAND-TO-HAND FIGHTER

Jazz is small for an Autobot, but uses his size to his advantage. He is fast, nimble, and fights with a tricky martial-arts style.

He was part of the original Autobot team who came to Earth with Optimus, and serves as First Lieutenant to the Autobot leader.

He bravely stood up to Megatron in Mission City, allowing several humans to escape, but the Decepticon leader's strength was too much for him and he was killed by Megatron.

HEIGHT: 15 FEET

POWER LEVEL 6

39

JOB

Autobot Lieutenant and assistant commander to Optimus Prime.

WEAPONS

Machine gun with tough shield behind it allows Jazz to fire and protect himself at the same time. Also special electromagnet means he can disarm enemies without harming them.

DISGUISE

Pontiac Solstice sports car. Like Jazz, it is fast, easy to manoeuvre and very cool!

STARSCREAM

KEY FACTS

DECEPTICON SECOND-IN-COMMAND

POWERFUL AIR-BASED TRANSFORMER

CUNNING AND DECEITFUL

CAN TRAVEL AT SUPERSONIC SPEEDS

Starscream is Megatron's right-hand man, but he is a sly Transformer, and given the chance would overthrow his master and lead the Decepticons himself.

Starscream led the Decepticons to Earth to rescue Megatron. He led the assault on the Hoover Dam that freed Megatron and unleashed the Transformers' war on Earth.

His alternate mode as an F-22 aeroplane means that Starscream is often first on the scene in battles. He can travel through the air at supersonic speeds, unlike slower land-based Transformers.

The Autobots have no air-based robot to match Starscream, so they are particularly vulnerable to his fierce attacks from the skies.

Starscream can use his aeroplane jets when in robot mode, meaning he can jump very high or even use them as a hover pack.

Starscream persuaded his master Megatron to escape at the end of the battle in Egypt, allowing them to return to the fight when Sentinel Prime is revived.

JOB

Decepticon second-in-command and air commander for Megatron's forces. He rules the Decepticons when Megatron isn't there, and leads attacks from the air with his missile launchers.

WEAPONS

Missile launchers for use in the air and on the ground; deadly spinning saw in his right arm; heavy machine gun. Starscream is particularly dangerous from above.

DISGUISE

F-22 Raptor fighter plane. This supersonic jet allows Starscream to travel the Earth very quickly, and also allows him to use his heavy weaponry from the air in battle.

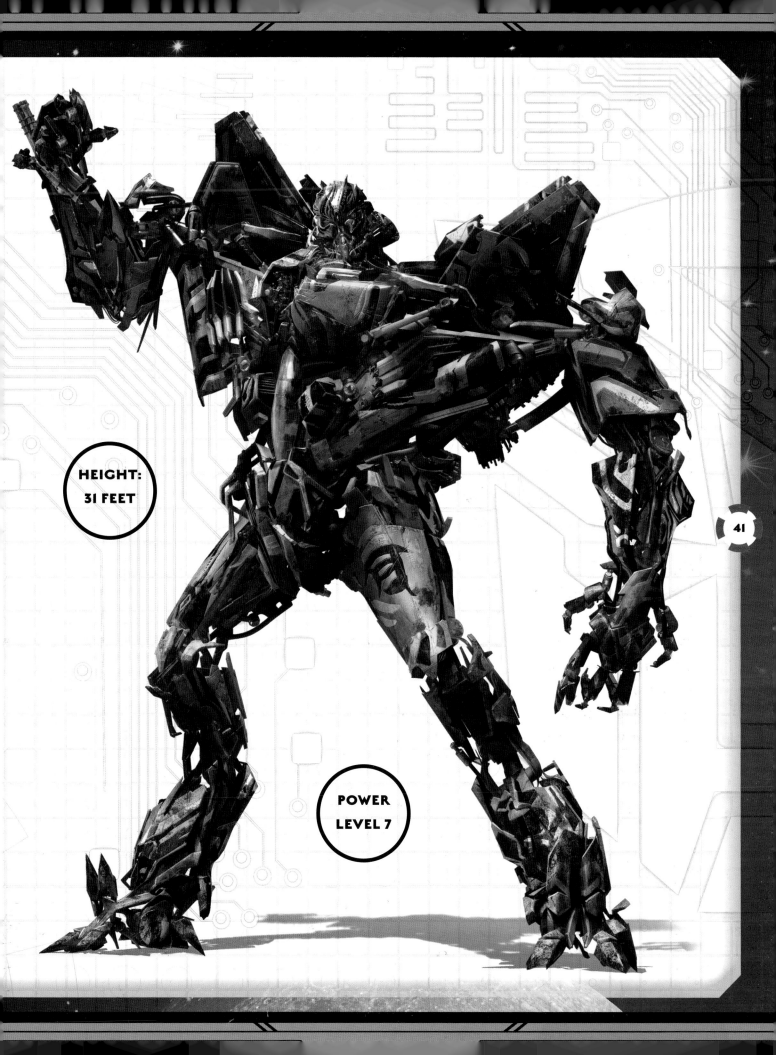

HEIGHT:
31 FEET

POWER
LEVEL 7

BARRICADE

KEY FACTS

FIERCE DECEPTICON SCOUT

DISGUISED AS CAR, UNLIKE MOST DECEPTICONS

DANGEROUS IN BATTLE

Unlike other Decepticons who don't disguise themselves as human vehicles, Barricade changes into a police car. This helps him blend in when hunting down targets.

Barricade's first scouting job on Earth was tracking down Sam and abducting him. Luckily, Bumblebee was on hand to fend him off...

Barricade and Bumblebee are about the same size and very evenly matched in battle. As they ripped into each other, neither Transformer could kill the other – although Bee did manage to escape with Sam unharmed.

JOB

Decepticon scout and warrior. Barricade seeks out targets on Earth, such as Sam, and is not afraid to attack if he thinks it will help the Decepticon cause.

WEAPONS

Spinning blade wheels in Barricade's hands make him a deadly enemy up close.

DISGUISE

Police car. This allows him to blend in with human traffic, which is essential for his scouting and tracking role.

HEIGHT: 16 FEET

POWER LEVEL 6

DEVASTATOR

KEY FACTS

VAST DESTRUCTIVE MONSTER

MADE UP OF SMALLER CONSTRUCTICONS

CAN LAY WASTE TO ANYTHING IN PATH

The biggest Decepticon yet, Devastator is a giant more than twice as big as Megatron or Optimus.

Devastator is made up of many small Constructicons, who combine together to form the massive beast. Megatron keeps tight control of Devastator as his brains don't match his muscle power!

Devastator's colossal strength was harnessed by Megatron when the top of the Great Pyramid needed ripping off to reveal the Star Harvester. Only a beast as strong as Devastator could have done the job.

JOB

Massive warrior to be called in when incredible strength and destruction is needed. Sheer size makes him very difficult to beat.

DISGUISE

Devastator breaks up into several smaller Constructicons, all of which are disguised as different construction vehicles.

WEAPONS

Terrifying Vortex Grinder in mouth that sucks enemies – and anything else – into its path. Also heavy missile launchers and several guns.

43

HEIGHT: 100 FEET

POWER LEVEL 10

TRANSFORMERS QUIZ

Are you an expert on the Transformers Universe? Take this tricky quiz to find out!

I. Which Transformer is Sam's personal bodyguard?
a) Sideswipe
b) Frenzy
c) Bumblebee

2. Which Decepticon freed Megatron by thawing him out?
a) Frenzy
b) Starscream
c) The Fallen

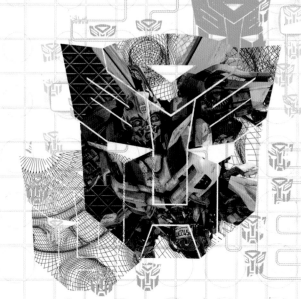

3. What is the name of the Transformers' home planet?
a) Cybertoria
b) Cybertron
c) Cyberwar

4. Where was Megatron frozen for thousands of years?
a) A freezer
b) Cybertron
c) The North Pole

5. What item is needed to fire the Star Harvester?
a) The Matrix of Leadership
b) The Sun Matrix
c) The Key of Leadership

6. Which Autobot defected to the Decepticons?
a) Optimus Prime
b) Sentinel Prime
c) Megatron

7. Which Decepticon has only one eye?
a) Devastator
b) Barricade
c) Shockwave

8. Where did the final battle for the AllSpark take place?
a) New York City
b) Mission City
c) Mexico City

9. Who is the Autobot weapons expert?
a) Ironhide
b) Bumblebee
c) Jazz

10. What is the name of the human/Autobot military unit?
a) TEST
b) NEST
c) WEST

Name that Transformer!
Can you tell which Transformer the details below are from?

1

2

3

4

5

6

TRANSFORMERS QUIZ

11.What is the name of the ex-Sector 7 agent who helps Sam and the US army?
a) Simmons
b) Simpson
c) Simple

12. Which two people below were brought back to life at the battle of the Star Harvester?
a) Optimus Prime
b) The Fallen
c) Sam

13. What creature does Shockwave have as a pet?
a) Cybertronian Tank
b) Cybertronian Crane
c) Cybertronian Driller

14. What is Devastator made up of?
a) Constructicons
b) The other Decepticons
c) Broken cars

15. Which two brothers tried vainly to bring down Devastator?
a) Skins and Hubcap
b) Skids and Mudflap
c) Wings and Handclap

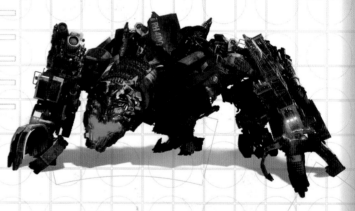

16. Which device teleports Cybertron right next to Earth?
a) TheWinged Bridge
b) The Space Hole
c) The Space Bridge

17. What is the special energy that powers Cybertron, and all Transformers, called?
a) Energizer
b) Energon
c) Cyberizer

18. What is Bumblebee's alternate mode?
a) A yellow Camaro
b) A green Camaro
c) A red Camaro

19. Which Autobot ship crashed on the moon?
a) The Boat
b) The Ship
c) The Ark

20. Who is the only Transformer who can bring others back to life?
a) Megatron
b) Sentinel Prime
c) Optimus Prime

Alternate Forms Puzzle
Match the Transformers below to their disguises! Draw lines to match them up.

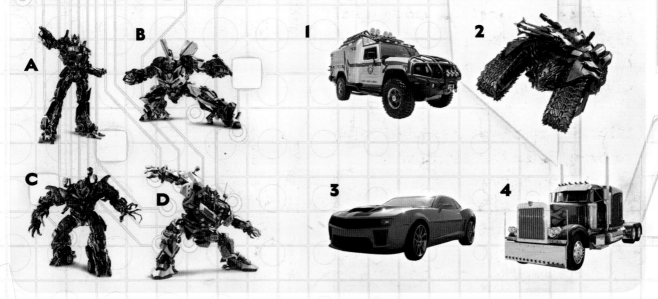

A
B
1
2
C
D
3
4

ANSWERS

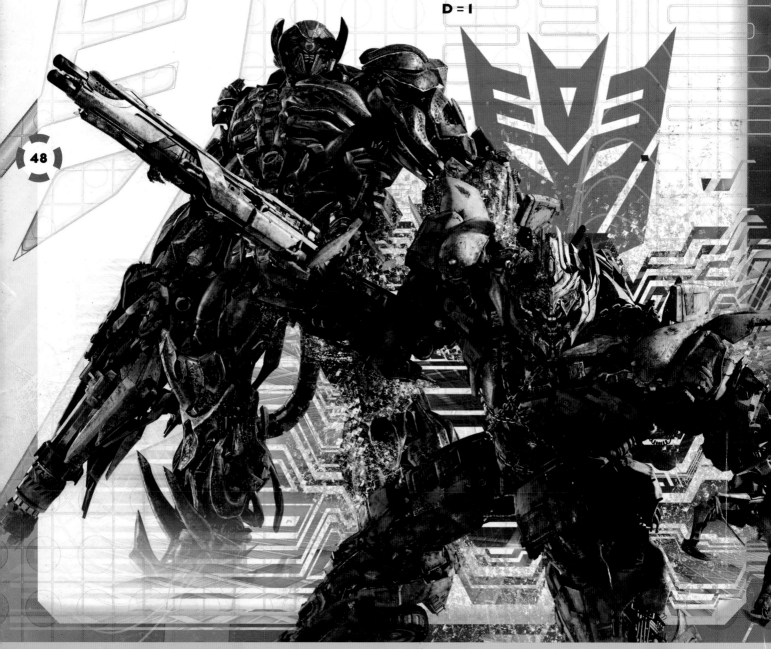

TRANSFORMERS QUIZ:

1 = c	**6** = b	**11** = a	**16** = c
2 = a	**7** = c	**12** = a, c	**17** = b
3 = b	**8** = b	**13** = c	**18** = a
4 = c	**9** = a	**14** = a	**19** = c
5 = a	**10** = b	**15** = b	**20** = c

NAME THAT TRANSFORMER:

1. Optimus Prime
2. Starscream
3. Ironhide
4. Megatron
5. The Fallen
6. Sentinel Prime

ALTERNATE FORMS PUZZLE:

A = 4

B = 3

C = 2

D = 1